Max's Fez

and

I am Izza

Whizz

Whizz

Whizz

Whizz

Written by
Kirsty Holmes

Illustrated by
Lynne Feng

Can you make it through the maze to collect the letter z? How many objects beginning with z can you collect along the way?

Max's Fez

and

I am Izza

PHASE 3

3a

Level 3 – Yellow

Helpful Hints for Reading at Home

The graphemes (written letters) and phonemes (units of sound) used throughout this series are aligned with Letters and Sounds. This offers a consistent approach to learning whether reading at home or in the classroom. Books levelled as 'a' are an introduction to this band. Readers can advance to 'b' where graphemes are consolidated and further graphemes are introduced.

HERE IS A LIST OF ALTERNATIVE GRAPHEMES FOR THIS PHASE OF LEARNING. AN EXAMPLE OF THE PRONUNCIATION CAN BE FOUND IN BRACKETS.

Phase 3			
j (jug)	v (van)	w (wet)	x (fox)
y (yellow)	z (zoo)	zz (buzz)	qu (quick)
ch (chip)	sh (shop)	th (thin/then)	ng (ring)
ai (rain)	ee (feet)	igh (night)	oa (boat)
oo (boot/look)	ar (farm)	or (for)	ur (hurt)
ow (cow)	oi (coin)	ear (dear)	air (fair)
ure (sure)	er (corner)		

HERE ARE SOME WORDS WHICH YOUR CHILD MAY FIND TRICKY.

Phase 3 Tricky Words			
he	you	she	they
we	all	me	are
be	my	was	her

HERE ARE SOME WORDS THAT MIGHT NOT YET BE FULLY DECODABLE.

Challenge Words			
zebra	frizzy	pink	

PHASE 3

3a

This book is an 'a' level and is a yellow level 3 book band.

Max's Fez

Illustrated by
Lynne Feng

Written by
Kirsty Holmes

I am Max. This is my fez.

My fez fits my fuzz!

In my pot, I mix and mix and mix.
I tap my fez.

The pot is buzzing! The pot is fizzing!

It is an elf. The elf fits in the pot.

That is my fez! No, elf!

An elf in a fez? No! Bad elf!

Look at the fez. Buzz! Fizz! Look at the elf. Zip! Zap!

Zip zop zap, get the fez back!

The elf is sad. This is my fez. It fits my fuzz.

The pot is buzzing! The pot is fizzing!

An elf fez is in the pot!

Can you say this sound and draw it with your finger?

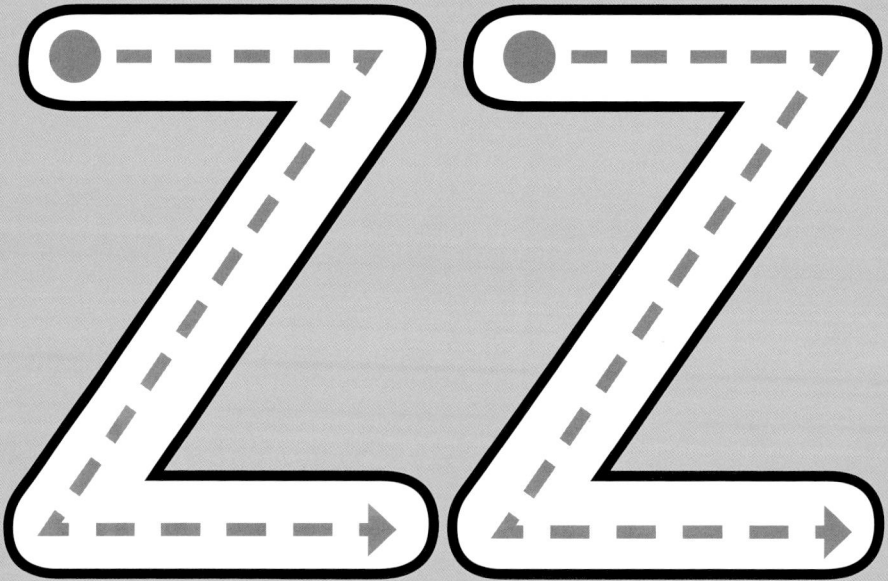

I am Izza

Written by
Kirsty Holmes

Illustrated by
Lynne Feng

Izza meets an ox.

Am I an ox?

The ox is big.

I am not
an ox.

Izza meets a fox.

Am I a fox?

The fox is red.

Izza meets a buzzing bee. Buzz!
Buzz!

The bee zigs and zags.

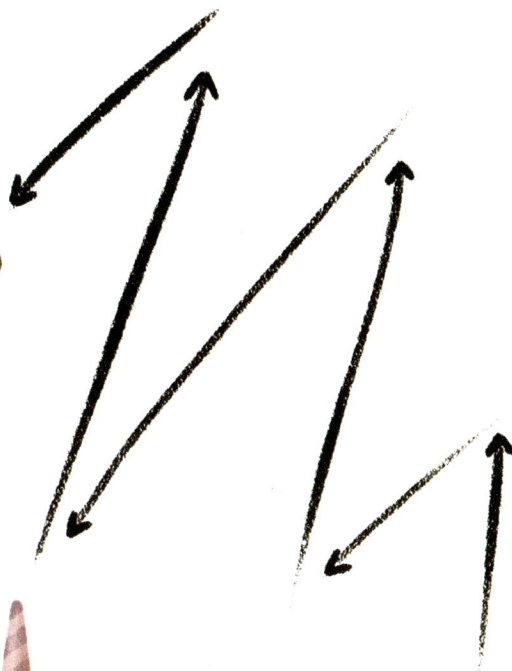

I am not a bee.

Izza meets a boxer dog.

Am I a boxer dog?

The boxer dog wags his tail.

I am not
a boxer dog.

Izza meets a zebra.

Am I a zebra?

The zebra is not pink.

I am not a zebra.

Izza is not an ox, a fox, a bee, a dog or a zebra.

Izza is pink. Izza has fuzz.

BookLife PUBLISHING

BookLife Readers

©2020 **BookLife Publishing Ltd.**
King's Lynn, Norfolk PE30 4LS

ISBN 978-1-83927-283-7

All rights reserved. Printed in Malaysia.
A catalogue record for this book is available
from the British Library.

Max's Fez & I am Izza
Written by Kirsty Holmes
Illustrated by Lynne Feng

An Introduction to BookLife Readers...

Our Readers have been specifically created in line with the London Institute of Education's approach to book banding and are phonetically decodable and ordered to support each phase of the Letters and Sounds document.

Each book has been created to provide the best possible reading and learning experience. Our aim is to share our love of books with children, providing both emerging readers and prolific page-turners with beautiful books that are guaranteed to provoke interest and learning, regardless of ability.

BOOK BAND GRADED using the Institute of Education's approach to levelling.

PHONETICALLY DECODABLE supporting each phase of Letters and Sounds.

EXERCISES AND QUESTIONS to offer reinforcement and to ascertain comprehension.

BEAUTIFULLY ILLUSTRATED to inspire and provoke engagement, providing a variety of styles for the reader to enjoy whilst reading through the series.

AUTHOR INSIGHT: KIRSTY HOLMES

Kirsty Holmes, holder of a BA, PGCE, and an MA, was born in Norfolk, England. She has written over 60 books for BookLife Publishing, and her stories are full of imagination, creativity and fun.

PHASE 3

3a

This book is an 'a' level and is a yellow level 3 book band.

Additional images courtesy of Shutterstock.com. p.4 – Maquiladora, KemarinSore, Kantri, Zonda, brgfx